MAGGO

ALSO BY PAUL MULDOON

New Weather 1973

Mules 1977

Why Brownlee Left 1980

Quoof 1983

Meeting the British 1987

Selected Poems 1968–1986 1987

Madoc: A Mystery 1990

The Annals of Chile 1994

Hay 1998

Poems 1968–1998 2001

Moy Sand and Gravel 2002

Horse Latitudes 2006

*The End of the Poem:
Oxford Lectures* 2006

MAGGOT

POEMS BY

PAUL **MULDOON**

FARRAR STRAUS GIROUX

NEW YORK

Farrar, Straus and Giroux
18 West 18th Street, New York 10011

Distributed in Canada by D&M Publishers, Inc.
Printed in the United States of America
Published in 2010 by Farrar, Straus and Giroux
First paperback edition, 2011

The Library of Congress has cataloged
the hardcover edition as follows:
Muldoon, Paul.
    Maggot : poems / Paul Muldoon.— 1st ed.
        p. cm.
    ISBN 978-0-374-20032-9 (hardcover : alk. paper)
    I. Title.

PR6063.U367M36 2010
821'.914—dc22

                                        2010005700

Paperback ISBN: 978-0-374-53301-4

Designed and composed by Quemadura

www.fsgbooks.com

1 3 5 7 9 10 8 6 4 2

FOR DOROTHY

CONTENTS

MAGGOT

PLAN B

On my own head be it if, after the years of elocution and
    pianoforte,
the idea that I may have veered

away from the straight
and narrow of Brooklyn or Baltimore for a Baltic state

is one at which, all things being equal, I would demur.
A bit like Edward VII cocking his ear

at the mention of Cork. Yet it seems I've managed nothing more
than to have fetched up here.

I I

To have fetched up here in Vilna—the linen plaids,
the amber, the orange-cap boletus

like a confession extorted from a birch,
the foot-wide pedestal upon which a prisoner would perch

on one leg in the former KGB headquarters
like a white stork

before tipping into a pool of icy water,
to be reinstated more than once by a guard with a pitchfork.

III

It was with a pitchfork they prodded Topsy, the elephant
that killed her keeper on Coney Island

when he tried to feed her a lit cigarette,
prodded her through Luna Park in her rain-heavy skirt

to where she would surely have been hanged by the neck
had the ASPCA not got themselves into such a lather

and Thomas Edison arrived in the nick
of time to greet the crowd he'd so long hoped to gather.

IV

I myself have been trying to gather the dope
from a KGB surveillance tape

on the Chazon Ish, "the wisest Jew alive," a master of the
   catchall
clause who was known to cudgel

his brains in a room high in a Vilna courtyard
on the etymology of "dork"

while proposing that the KGB garotte
might well be a refinement of the Scythian torc.

v

The Scythian torc had already been lent a new lease
of life as the copper wire with which Edison would splice

Topsy to more than 6,000 volts of alternating current,
though not before he'd prepared the ground

with a boatload of carrots laced with cyanide.
This was 1903. The year in which Edward VII paid

out a copper line from his mustachioed snout
to the electric chair where Edison himself was now belayed.

VI

Now a belayed, bloody prisoner they've put on the spot
and again and again zapped

is the circus rider on a dappled
croup from which he's more than once toppled

into the icy water, spilling his guts
about how his grandfather had somehow fetched up in Cork

straight from the Vilna ghetto,
having misheard, it seems, "Cork" for "New York."

VII

For New York was indeed the city in which the floor teetered
at a ball thrown in 1860 in honor of Edward

(then Prince of Wales), the city in which even I may have put
myself above all those trampled underfoot,

given my perfect deportment all those years I'd skim
over the dying and the dead

looking up to me as if I might at any moment succumb
to the book balanced on my head.

GEESE

Like suitors whom we once held in exaggeratedly high regard,
these geese have so long been on permanent loan
we take them for granted, knowing they'll no more run
    themselves ragged
on the Christmas lawn

than spill their guts at an inaugural.
That our grandfathers dipped geese feet in a mix of tar
and sawdust may seem cruel
till we remember it was meant to save some wear and tear

on the long road to the mart.
I look up to see a dozen geese balk at the hurdle
of finding caraway *and* fresh coriander

and am tempted to think they're still weighing the odds of
    being mired
in our most lackluster of zones against putting a girdle
about the earth with Santa and his reindeer.

Our ornamental reindeer, while they may not urinate on
    demand,
are at least anatomically correct.
The geese, however, are offered in atonement
for a delivery system that had creaked

along before skidding to a halt. I look up to count fourteen
when a mere twelve
were on order—six in viridian,
six in blue delf.

The Christmas lawn? That's to say "aerodrome."
Though they're still set to hobble from furrow to Bronze Age
    furrow,
they're cognizant of the psychological

interpretation of Penelope's dream
in which a squadron of their kind was given a thorough
trouncing by an eagle.

III

The idea being the Odysseus-eagle proves to the geese-suitors
that, when they courted his queen,
they were courting disaster.
A porcelain doll will tell you no amount of cayenne

applied to a wound on a trial basis
can possibly staunch
the flow of blood. Still appearing under their own auspices
as a sky still somewhere turns on its hinge.

I look up as my friend once looked up
to behold his son sleepwalking from rafter to rafter
of the unfinished cabin. The very one. Bartholomew.

I, too, am tempted to whoop
a warning but think better of it, falling in after
yet another goose with its standard-issue, chin-strapped pith
    helmet.

MORE GEESE

Now the sweep of the wing of a goose that had broken a child's
   arm
with a flying tackle
on the next-but-one farm
was cut short as the Romans had planned to cut the cackle

of the geese on the Capitoline Hill
and utilized by the slattern
turned spick-and-span housewife to dust her sill.
They must be sacred still to some deity, these geese in a
   holding pattern

over the same pharmaceutical company's front lawn
on which their ancestors were staked
till their calls,

we hear, had drawn
down more geese flying north, must ache still as their
   ancestors ached
for the chance to fend off a night attack by the Gauls.

A CHRISTMAS IN THE FIFTIES

FOR RICHARD WILBUR

It was Charles Barrett in his *Wild Life of Australia and New Guinea*
who inspired her devotion to Pelorus Jack, the pilot dolphin of
    Cook Strait,
The Infant Jesus now having been airlifted in a canister
to supply the rank and file
in heathen Indochina, my mother in turn offering me the skinny
on how our eternal reward would be commensurate
with the trials of this vale of tears in which even Roger Bannister
was doomed to rerun the four-minute mile
against not only a river that disembogues
into a gulf of which it could hitherto merely have dreamt
but also the crew of SS *Penguin*, one of those assorted rogues
having made an assassination attempt
on Pelorus Jack himself, after which the dolphin would give a
    wide berth
to the *Penguin* alone of all the ships of earth.

SANDRO BOTTICELLI:

THE ADORATION OF THE MAGI

GOLD

A sky of china clay in which something very like a star
flared as over Bethlehem
and where the Star
of the Sea herself was obscured by a plume

of ox breath. Christmas Eve. My mother boiling onions for sage
and onion stuffing. The tinsel
bought in Omagh from an Eastern sage
who still went door-to-door. My Christmas handsel

merely an orange against which I now began to bray
as the gallbladder brays against its own mass.
This was an orange that would taste of mud juice,

an orange I would fling over the hedge near McParland's Brae
on my way to midnight Mass
with a largesse rarely seen since the days of the Medicis.

FRANKINCENSE

Since the days of the Medicis there had been little or no change
in the way an acolyte
like myself held back some loose change
from the collection box. A brass farthing was as good as gold

to an altar boy harboring his incense boat
or a thurible its robin glow. A mere two days till the wren
would be in the same boat
as the bittern. A mere two days of torrential rain

till the jenny wren flew
the coop. What I wanted was cash on the barrel
rolled out by a Sisyphean

Santa Claus who would survive being briefly at the mercy of
   our flue
as surely as the downpour the drainpipe once held over a barrel
was now the water in the saucepan.

MYRRH

Now the water in the saucepan was off the boil
my mother would turn, spluttering, from the can of kaolin
she was about to apply to a boil
on the back of my neck to clean

the surrounding area. The icing on the cake. These tears of gum
on the Christmas tree the closest we'd as yet come to myrrh,
though tincture of myrrh was still prescribed for gum
and mouth disorders. Christmas Eve. A mere

two days till the hunters would raise the puss,
a pack of hounds starting it from its form
and following it through the surrounding area till, jingle-jangle,

its nozzle would fill with blood. As yet, a little bloody pus
on this morning's poultice gauze the closest we'd come to the
    form
of a star halted in a sky of china clay.

A HARE AT ALDERGROVE

A hare standing up at last on his own two feet
in the blasted grass by the runway may trace his lineage to the
 great
assembly of hares that, in the face of what might well have
 looked like defeat,
would, in 1963 or so, migrate
here from the abandoned airfield at Nutt's Corner, not long
 after Marilyn Monroe
overflowed from her body stocking
in *Something's Got to Give*. These hares have themselves so long
 been given to row
against the flood that when a King
of the Hares has tried to ban bare knuckle fighting, so wont
are they to grumble and gripe
about what will be acceptable and what won't
they've barely noticed that the time is ripe
for them to shake off the din
of a pack of hounds that has caught their scent
and take in that enormity just as I've taken in
how my own DNA is 87% European and East Asian 13%.
So accustomed had they now grown
to a low-level human hum that, despite the almost weekly
 atrocity
in which they'd lost one of their own

to a wheeled blade, they followed the herd towards this eternal
   city
as if they'd had a collective change of heart.
My own heart swells now as I watch him nibble on a shoot
of blaeberry or heather while smoothing out a chart
by which he might divine if our Newark-bound 757 will one
   day overshoot
the runway about which there so often swirled
rumors of Messerschmitts.
Clapper-lugged, cleft-lipped, he looks for all the world
as if he might never again put up his mitts
despite the fact that he shares a Y chromosome
with Niall of the Nine Hostages,
never again allow his om
to widen and deepen by such easy stages,
never relaunch his campaign as melanoma has relaunched its
   campaign
in a friend I once dated,
her pain rising above the collective pain
with which we've been inundated
as this one or that has launched an attack
to the slogan of "Brits Out" or "Not an Inch"
or a dull ack-ack
starting up in the vicinity of Ballynahinch,
looking for all the world as if he might never again get into a
   fluster
over his own entrails,

never again meet luster with luster
in the eye of my dying friend, never establish what truly ails
another woman with a flesh wound
found limping where a hare has only just been shot, never again
    bewitch
the milk in the churn, never swoon as we swooned
when Marilyn's white halter-top dress blew up in *The Seven*
    Year Itch,
in a flap now only as to whether
we should continue to tough it out till
something better comes along or settle for this salad of
    blaeberry and heather
and a hint of common tormentil.

MORYSON'S FANCY

A most horrible spectacle of three children (whereof the eldest was not
above ten years old), all eating and gnawing with their teeth the entrails
of their mother, upon whose flesh they had fed 20 days past, and having
eaten all from the feet upward to the bare bones, roasting it continually
by a slow fire, were now come to the eating of her said entrails in like
sort roasted, yet not divided from the body, being as yet raw.

FYNES MORYSON, *An History of Ireland,*
From the Year 1599 to 1603 (1617)

Let the hare sit, my father would mutter, as if to a dog
that has slunk in with the fog
and lies with one ear cocked to three crickets
on the hearth. Not only are all three children suffering from
    rickets
but one's so bowlegged we might divine
a ceremonial arch
under which a legion will form a triumphal line
after the unprecedented forced march

by which it put paid to some far-flung Celtic burgh.
A hare running to the left as in the exergue
of a Celtic coin will be seen by Boudicca as an omen
of her prevailing against the Roman
army even now massed on the wold.

These three children for whom their mother at first seemed
     asleep
may have known a hare running to the right from a fold
of her skirt would have them leap

into an inauspicious stretch of Fermanagh bog
where generation after generation would learn to mich and cog
rather than follow their callings as scholars.
Check out the cuffs. Check out the collars.
Check out the flesh farthingales
through which they so resolutely ate.
Maybe they'll yet look into their mother's entrails
and somehow haruspicate

that the Muldoons will lose their hold on the ancient barony of
     Lurg
and be reduced to ferrying pilgrims to Lough Derg.
Maybe they'll be forewarned also of how to tackle
this most horrible spectacle
of themselves as a synonym
for savagery, a stain
on the integrity of the nation, for while they acted on a whim
their whim will nonetheless sustain

the will of generation after generation through the hard slog,
allowing them to pillage an estate or prog
an apple orchard as casually as the Blennerhassets

would finally strip the Muldoons of their assets.
I find myself heart-hurt
by the iffy inevitability of it
now Boudicca has loosed a hare from the fold of her skirt
where another might easily have let the hare sit.

THE FISH LADDER

Forty years since I proved a micher
and ate blackberries
along the plank road by a dilapidated weir
that had somehow failed to pave
the way from being a local eyesore

to something on which we might rest assured,
a corduroy causey thrown down by Caesar
across the Fens
being cut and dried by comparison.
Though a flax dam

in which our enthusiasm may be damped
as we grope
towards clarity with the high-strung
sea trout and salmon
is not to be confused with the bog hole

in which my father proved a last ditcher
during World War II, a flax dam may be the very
pool in which we find ourselves in the clear.
Less and less, though, will bog water stave
off the great gobs of gore

that come and go like Jonah's gallows gourd
from the wound where a doctor still views his tweezer
through the lens
of day-to-day life in a Roman garrison.
Even Jonah had run himself ragged as he swam

against the workload with which he'd been swamped
those last few months in the hope,
I expect, of skipping a rung.
Sometimes the more we examine
things, the less we understand our dual role

as proven escape artist and proven identity switcher.
Just look at how two ferries
have gone down within plain sight of the pier
but only one tatterdemalion wave
has managed to stumble ashore.

LATERAL

In the province of Gallia Narbonensis and the
region of Nemausus there is a marsh called Latera
where dolphins and men co-operate to catch fish.

PLINY THE ELDER, *Natural History*

In spite of a dolphin wearing through, every two hours, his
    outer layer
of conveyor-belt polymer, in spite of the spill of venom
by which his affiliates used to lure
mullet into their nets having taken its course
through his veins, he simply won't hear of how his affiliates
    outsource
their dirty work to another ring of the plenum.

Even the blue heron may backpedal
as he pins a medal
to his uniformed chest while vaunting cutoff denims,
yet a dolphin won't rethink his having left it to men
to send mixed signals to the mullahs they processed in some
    holding pen.

QUAIL

Forty years in the wilderness
of Antrim and Fermanagh
where the rime would deliquesce
like tamarisk-borne manna

and the small-shot of hail
was de-somethinged. Defrosted.
This is to say nothing of the flocks of quail
now completely exhausted

from having so long entertained an
inordinately soft spot for the hard man
like Redmond O'Hanlon or Roaring Hanna

who delivers himself up only under duress
after forty years in the wilderness
of Antrim and Fermanagh.

WHEN THE PIE WAS OPENED

I

Every morning the water again runs clear
as it has for twenty years
of jabs
and stabs
where we've joined in single combat, my dear,

on a strand or at a ford.
Every evening I've fleshed my sword
in a scabbard.
The hedgehog bristling on your tabard.
Behind each of us is arrayed a horde

of heroes ready to vie
for a piece of the pie
with Hector, Ajax, Ferdia, Cuchulainn,
and all the other squeaky-clean
champions who've once more forgotten to die.

11

Once more forgotten to engage
in the campaign to raise their minimum wage
now all their checks are dud.
So much for a crossarm stained with blood
being enough to refresh the page

like a sword exposing a bone.
My own reputation already fly-blown
when we took that trip
in the coupé. I must have been setting my Darby
against your Joan

complete with chemo-chemise
when we passed those sentries shooting the breeze
at Canal and Mulberry,
our minds still chaste and our hearts still pure
and the moon still saying cheese.

III

Forgotten to die like the cancer cells
in their pell-mell
through an escutcheon fesse.
The hot compress
on a pustule from which the pus wells

as it welled for Job.
Every evening the impulse to disrobe
and take a little potsherd
to scrape the skin off whatever we've butchered.
Was there really a probe

into whether or not you would stand the test
of taking a hedgehog for your crest?
As if you might gather
yourself about a core
of high explosives packed into a vest.

IV

A vest opened now like a dossier.
A badger with a white line running all the way
back from its snout.
Would that the world were indeed to be broken out
of its crust like a hedgehog baked in clay

by Gypsies at the end of a lane.
Would that it were to hang from a crane.
The steam rising through a slash
where we've made a hash
of the whole thing. As for the bloodstain

on the crossarm,
somebody told me vinegar works a charm.
Lifts off the whole kit
and caboodle like a pheasant at last making good
its escape from a pheasant farm.

V

A pheasant farm where we watched a pheasant's ascent
translate into a dent
on our automobile. Wham.
I bet they could make out even on the jam-cam
steam rising from the vent

of a wound dressed with sphagnum moss.
Bosom-boss.
The white line running all the way from the badger
to the gamekeeper-turned-poacher
who really couldn't give a toss

about having to share
her champion's portion of Brie or Camembert.
The minor obsession with glitz
from a major klutz
who's found herself enmeshed in a snare.

32

VI

A snare through which I myself might squeeze
on my hands and knees
to nuzzle your butt.
Your hair *à la garçonne*. Your urchin cut
softened by a garland of heartsease

and woundwort.
That your olive-drab body in a shirt
of olive drab
would be sufficient, after your radiotherapy,
to trigger a dirty bomb alert

at Canal and Mulberry sets the stage
for another twinge of the gauge
on my own instrument bank.
Another heart-pang
neither badger nor hedgehog grease may assuage.

VII

A snare in which we find ourselves enmeshed
as every evening our swords are fleshed
while Hector and Ajax
apply flax
and white of eggs. The page is refreshed,

my dear, only as our servants bind
our wounds. A rind
closing over the Camembert or Brie
in some fancy hostelry
where we've wined and dined

in anticipation of putting on our gear
and steeling ourselves for the belly spear.
The shit storm
through a bloody stream
in which every morning the water again runs clear.

THE WINDSHIELD

I

My breath is furring a windshield
where I sit in my windcheater,
engine shut off, jolted by a rearview mirror's jolt,
and wait for my daughter

to be released from her rehearsal.
A production of *Much Ado*
in which she's taking the part of Ursula.
All at once I recognize that shadow

coming towards me as my own, all at once
recognize the Cathedral car park
where my mother has sat

while I've been impressed by *The Pirates of Penzance*
or held forth in a debate, coming through the dark
to find her turned the wrong side out.

II

To find her turned the wrong side out
like a birch relieved of its bark,
a custom relieved of its consuetude,
would be to avail myself of this opportunity to remark

on the pros or cons
of the death penalty or animal captivity
or integrated education.
This house proposes that we are slaves of duty.

This house proposes that we not sully
the memory of a parent, least of all one who sends a judder
through a child,

unleashing rather that satin-lined grizzly,
that selfsame man-eater
whose breath is furring the windshield.

FRANÇOIS BOUCHER:

ARION ON THE DOLPHIN

I

A rock god waiting in the wings
to set himself before the king,
this eye-linered and lip-glossed Arion fouters
with his lyre's five strings

across the span
of twenty-five centuries. His big hair's bigger than ever from
    the fan
of a wind machine. The sky's pinks and pewters
resound in the brainpan

of a bloodied Triton still grasping his horn
through a brine flurry
while the doo-wop chorus

of Nereids or such sea-born
nymphs seem content to hold their hurry
till those twenty-five centuries have taken their course.

A course that was laid long before the keel of oak
was laid to soak
in Piraeus, got to be, long before murrey
would infiltrate his cloak,

the mulberry over which Arion will mull
long after a Triton's skull
explodes. Not to worry, he'll muse, not to worry
if the top-heavy hull

is shortly a hulk through which they'll pick
as they'll pick through the rubble
of the Depository elevator shaft. What's not to love about the
    Teflon,

its nonstick
complete with the dead giveaway of a three-day stubble
on the cheek of a dolphin?

III

Less dolphin this than dog, dog-paddling through drifts of brine,
bearing a keg of brandy wine
for lost sea mountaineers. Less dolphin than double
of the figurehead of the ship in sharp decline

behind him, this sudden displacement of teak
suggesting the outlook's bleak
for both dolphin and *Dauphin*, spelling trouble
for another figurehead who'll soon barely squeak

through the ranks of sansculottes
and the tumbrils' rough-and-tumble
to die in a shitty kennel

at the age of ten, a boy king going down at a rate of knots
through the scumble
of pewter and pink on a distant grassy knoll.

IV

On a grassy knoll two Tritons dressed as tramps
are doing the Versailles vamp
while, high above the rumble,
another is aiming to put his stamp

on something, anything. The Nereid as a flitch
of halibut, caught without a stitch
on this holiest of days. Not to worry if we fumble
as we bait and switch

in a storm sewer that might turn a mill
never mind a rumor mill. In a bit of a pickle,
that Nereid, who shows such pluck

before the likelihood of everything going downhill
like the trickle
of blood from a, got to be, butcher block.

v

Not to worry if the butcher massaging the rump
of a Nereid is *le boucher*, plumping and plumping the very clump
at which he'll prickle.
The Triton in a slump

across the raft has taken a hit
to the throat. The Nereid who's lost her kit
and might once have been up for a little slap and tickle
may now never know just how interknit

are herself and the lymph
in which her hair streams like a, got to be, streamer.
What's not to love about this vestige

of the tail of a water nymph
who might learn within the week it's not the blue-green of a
    scaly femur
but gangrene kicking into its second stage?

VI

The second stage where the rock god needs to simultaneously
   touch
and turn away from those who need to clutch
at him while crowding him out. What's not to love about a
   steamer
going down and, insomuch

as we may deduce if night will bring release
from his tribulations and his safe return to Greece,
about a Triton torn between nuzzling the calf of his redeemer
and gnawing it, this raft now being of a piece

with the raft of the *Medusa* and the raft
of the sunk PT-109, though neither he nor his fellow trumpet-
   tooters
may ever begin to drag out

the connection between the elevator shaft
and the storm sewer where the third of the shooters
waits in the wings for the motorcade?

MAGGOT

I used to wait on a motorcade
to stretch to the world rim.
Now I've been left in the shade
with only this slim jim.

I used to wait for a moonless night
before parachuting in.
Now it's come to light
I've spread myself too thin

where I'm waiting for some lover
to kick me out of bed
for having acted on a whim

when the yarrow opened its two-page spread
and the trout stirred from its hover
under a brook brim.

11

I used to wait for the dawn raid
where gloom gave way to glim
and packed the parachute I'd paid
out like the flim-

flammable box kite
of a wild boar's intestine.
Often an acolyte
will be taking it on the chin

where I'm waiting for some lover
to kick me out of bed
for having acted on a whim

in the scriptorium I fled
when a limestone coffer
was let slip by two seraphim.

III

I used to wait, undaunted, undismayed,
where one trout held on like grim
death to a frayed
leader while another would skim

the Personals in the hope she might ignite
the fire within.
Now I've taken the fight
to an identical twin

where I'm waiting for some lover
to kick me out of bed
for having acted on a whim

with the aforesaid
trout who was all in a pother
while pretending to be prissy-prim.

IV

I used to be somewhat swayed
by an Italian patronym.
Now the Val Cordevole brigade
holds firm at the gym.

I used to have an appetite
for wild boar in gin.
Now I take a sound bite
with a mic on a tiepin

where I'm waiting for some lover
to kick me out of bed
for having acted on a whim

with that Miss Trifoglio who led
me to believe I'd be "in clover"
now her main ingredient was Pimm's.

v

I used to wait in the colonnade
while a poplar got a trim
or watched as a partisan was flayed
with such vigor and vim

it no longer seemed a fancy-flight
to fancy my arm a fin.
Now I'm buoyant despite
having taken another tailspin

where I'm waiting for some lover
to kick me out of bed
for having acted on a whim,

her tongue livid with pencil lead
like the partisan I knew as a pencil shover
who dangles still by one limb.

VI

I used to admire a peasant maid
through her dimity-dim.
Now I ply my trade
in the interim

between dropping into the Dolomites
on a clandestine
mission and the breach site
I've yet to win

where I'm waiting for some lover
to kick me out of bed
for having acted on a whim

as unpremeditatedly as the pretty pre-med
who proved to be such a pushover
now she'd passed her prelims.

VII

I used to wait for the serenade
of a fly choir singing a fly hymn
without the visual aid
of the rubric some monk might limn

from carmine and graphite
bound in albumin.
Now I'm content to write
to her next of kin

where I'm waiting for some lover
to kick me out of bed
for having acted on a whim,

having been given up for dead
like so many left to smother
behind a chemise scrim.

VIII

I used to wait while a trout inveighed
against the yarrow corymb
as the birch will upbraid
the fly agaric with which it has a sym-

biotic relationship. Has-been is tight
with has-been.
An ex-Franciscan will plight
his troth to an ex-Ursuline

where I'm waiting for some lover
to kick me out of bed
for having acted on a whim

and quibbled with Miss Trifoglio instead
of taking up the offer
of her little Commie quim.

IX

I used to wait for another ambuscade
with only my hotwire shim.
Now I'm no less a blade
than Pistol, Bardolph or Nym.

I used to think the partisans wore white
because they were free of sin.
Now I think it only right
to have got beneath her skin

where I'm waiting for some lover
to kick me out of bed
for having acted on a whim

when she herself has taken it into her head
all those who've gone undercover
may as well sink as swim.

NOPE

It's not just another leper who can walk backwards while
    conducting a tour
and making a case for Lincoln's suspension of habeas corpus.
The wet collodion process followed photogravure
only in the way a ship follows a porpoise.
It's not, in fact, a mermaid but a porpoise of some kind
that seems to be throwing caution to every wind that blows.
My own terms are so ill defined
it's not just another leper whose arms are out at the elbows.
It's not that the lichen is an absolute indicator
of air pollution but it's more reliable than the pigmy sperm
    whale.
The Art Museum's Celtic gold stater
with its disjointed horse is completely off the scale.
It's not only some upperclassman who's misappropriated the
    weather vane.
It's not just another leper who's lost the gift of pain.

THE ROWBOAT

Every year he'd sunk
the old, clinker-built rowboat
so it might again float.
Every year he'd got drunk

as if he might once and for all write off
every year he'd sunk,
kerplunk, kerplunk,
one after another into a trough

no water would staunch.
Like a waterlogged tree trunk,
every year he'd sunk
just as he was about to launch

into a diatribe on the chunk
of change this bitch
was costing him, the debt into which
every year he'd sunk.

II

The old, clinker-built rowboat
with its shriveled strakes
would be immersed in the lake,
the lake that itself rewrote

many a stage play for the big screen.
The old, clinker-built rowboat
in which he'd stashed the ice tote
from L.L.Bean

for Crested Ten on the rocks
(one part Crested Ten, two parts creosote),
the old, clinker-built rowboat
he'd threatened to leave on the dock

and give a coat
of varnish that would somehow clinch the deal,
that would once and for all seal
the old, clinker-built rowboat.

III

So it might again float
the possibility one must expand
with Coutts and Co. (without the ampersand),
misquoting them as one might misquote

the price of Paramount stock
so it might again float.
More than once he'd written a promissory note
and put himself in hock

more than once to assuage
the fears for a property expressed by the Coutthroats
so it might again float
from the big screen to the stage

and gain by losing something of its bloat,
taking as he did the chance
it might be imbued with some new significance
so it might again float.

Every year he'd got drunk
and railed at this one and that,
the baseball birdbrain, the basketball gnat,
the gin-soaked punk

he threatened with a punching out of lights
every year he'd got drunk,
the Coutts & Co. quidnunc
whose argument was no more watertight

than any by which he might inure
himself against the basketball gnat's slam dunk.
Every year he'd got drunk
but resisted taking a cure

just as every year he'd shrunk
from the thought, kerpow,
he'd most likely go under given how
every year he'd got drunk.

MY LORD BYRON'S MAGGOT

Now the carp were nibbling at our foot soles
in a spa near Washington, we'd give a wide berth to the shoals
of brownie and blondie and lemon bar

and take on board a whole new set of goals
as we roved out along this firewalker's bed of orange-black coals
from the Motivational Seminar.

LINES FOR THE CENTENARY OF

THE BIRTH OF SAMUEL BECKETT

I

Only now do we see how each crossroads
was bound to throw up not just a cross
but a couple of gadabouts with goads,
a couple of gadabouts at a loss

as to why they were at the beck and call
of some old crock soaring above the culch
of a kitchen midden at evenfall,
some old crock roaring across the gulch

as a hanged man roars out to a hanged man.
Now bucket nods to bucket of the span
of an ash yoke, or something of that ilk . . .

Now one hanged man kicks at the end of his rope
in another little attack of hope.
Now a frog in one bucket thickens the milk.

11

Now a frog in one bucket thickens the milk
as it tries out for the sublime
from chime to birch-wood chime,
a frog thrown in with no more thought as to whilk

way he was geen
from the hussy turned resourceful housewife
than she gave to where in Ayreshire or Fife
her beloved spalpeen

might fetch up as a tatie-hoker,
a tatie-hoker revealing a lining of red tatted silk
to his sackcloth, so to speak,

just as it's revealed our stockbroker
is creaming off five hundred a week
while the frog in one bucket thickens the milk.

III

Now a frog in one bucket thickens the milk
as a heart might quicken behind its stave
at the thought of a thief who bilked
us of our life savings himself being saved.

Only now do we see . . . How spasm and lull
are mirrored somewhat by lull and spasm
when the nitwit roars out to the numbskull
thinking he might yet narrow the chasm

between his own cask and the other's keg,
thinking he might take the other down a peg
if not leave him completely in the lurch . . .

Leave him to ponder if it's less an ash
yoke tipped by his bucket of balderdash,
less an ash yoke than a crossbar of birch.

IV

Less an ash yoke than a crossbar of birch
from the single birch that insinuated itself into the grove
of oaks sacred to Jove
and took him in as from his perch

the nincompoop who's churning our account
took in the other knucklehead
with the proposal that our aversion to being bled
is pretty much tantamount

to the old crock being averse to paying his ransom,
the bucket where you would search
for the significance of a frog taking the plunge

proving to be less cask than keg, the transom
from which the old crock offered his vinegar sponge
less an ash yoke than a crossbar of birch.

Less an ash yoke than a crossbar of birch
and a birch-wood bucket where a frog breasts
the very milk we feared it would besmirch.
Only now do we see we're at the behest

not of some old crock kicking the beam
but ourselves. We balk at the idea, balk
at the idea of a frog no sooner opening a seam
in milk than it's . . . Surely not *caulked*?

Only now do we see how it's ourselves who skim
determinedly through the dim
of evenfall with no more regard for our load

as we glance up through the sky hoop
than the ninny who roars back to the nincompoop,
"Only now do we see how each crossroads . . ."

CHARLES BAUDELAIRE:

"THE ALBATROSS"

About one-third of all albatross chicks die on Midway, many as the
result of being mistakenly fed plastic by their parents. . . . Many
albatrosses are found to have swallowed disposable cigarette lighters—
which look remarkably similar to their staple food of squid.

BBC NEWS

Again and again, for a little light relief, the crew pulls in and
    pinions
an albatross, one of those great ocean-
going birds that are effortless companions
to a ship attempting the abyss by its own effortless motion.
Barely has he been flung down on the planks
than this Lord of the Blue is lamed and ashamed; he piddles
along with two white wings hanging from his flanks
like a pitiable pair of paddles.
This winged voyager, how unwieldy he is, how weak!
No time ago we found only felicity; now we find only fault.
One crewman forces a dudeen into his beak.
Another mimics the former highflier who's now all but halt.
The Poet is not unlike this Prince of the Clouds
who rode out the storm and suffered the slings
and arrows; exiled on dry land, amid the jeering crowds,
again and again he's dragged down by the weight of those wings.

THE HUMORS OF HAKONE

I

A corduroy road over a quag had kept me on the straight and
    narrow.
Now something was raising a stink.
A poem decomposing around what looked like an arrow.
Her stomach contents ink.

Too late to cast about for clues
either at the *purikura*, or "sticker-photo booth," or back at the
    Pagoda.
Too late to establish by autolysis, not to speak of heat loss,
the precise time of death on the road to Edo.

Who knew "forensic" derived from *forum*,
which senator's sword sealed the deal?
All I had to go on was this clog she'd taken as her platform,
this straight and narrow hair, this panty-hose heel.

I thought of how I'd once been inclined to grub
through the acidic soil
for a panty-hose toe or some such scrap
of evidence. Whereas Mount Fuji had yet to come to a head
    like a boil

64

about to crown its career,
it was too late to extrapolate from the cooling rate of fat
in a mortuary drawer
the rate of cooling in a body that threw off merely this sticker
   photo.

It was now far too late to know if this was even the scene of the
    crime.
Too late to ascertain from the serial number of a breast implant
if this was the same girl I'd seen in the *purikura* near the tearoom
back in Kyoto. Too late to determine if a salivary gland

might have secreted its critical enzyme
or, as her belly resumed its verdure,
implored an eye to give up its vitreous potassium
as a nun from a mendicant order

might unthinkingly draw in her voluminous
yellow robe to implore one for a little buckwheat.
Too late to put one's head into the noose
of the world as into the air pocket

of a capsized boat and swab the vitreous humor
off an eyeball. I'd read somewhere that the Japanese love of kitsch
is nowhere more
evident than in the craze for these sticker-photo booths which

go even further to reinforce
not only the heels of panty hose worn under a kimono
but the impression that phosphorus
might still be a common element in flash photography. Dead
common.

III

Too late to determine how long the girl I'd also glimpsed at the
    hot spring
had been beleaguered by pupae.
By day four the skin would have peeled from her thigh like a fine-
    mesh stocking.
I thought of *De Mundi Transitu*. Columbanus at Bobbio.

I thought of how I'd planned not to keep my end of the bargain
I drew up over that little cup of char
back in the Kyoka Ryokan.
I'd promised then I would willingly abjure

my right to eat globefish later that night in Santora
and enjoy my own little brush
with death. Too late to determine in which mountain sanitaria
the lepers had in fact been held. Too late to ascertain if Roshi

belonged to the Tokugawa clan with their triple-hollyhock mon
and their boat laid up for winter in shrink-wrap.
Who knew that *humus* might lie beneath "humane"?
Too late to deduce if the father of this girl in her geisha robe

had met her mother on the main drag
of Waxahachie, Texas, while he worked on the Superconducting
   Super Collider.
Too late to scour the scene for a kimono swatch or a toe rag
to send back to the lab for a culture.

It was far too late to have forsworn
my ambition to eat globefish in an attempt to buck this tiresome
    trend
towards peace and calm. Too late to establish if the shorn
head of a mendicant nun might send

a signal back to the father of the girl I glimpsed on the Tokaido
    line
who had himself worked on the antilock
braking system of the bullet train. Too late to find a chalk outline
never mind the metallic

smell of blood on the corduroy
road to Edo. Too late for this girl to release an endorphin
to allow her to brave the *nishikigoi*,
or "braided carp," which might have been the only ones to raven

on her foot soles. At Ryoan-ji a monk must rake and re-rake
the gravel with a birch-wood tine
till it looks like a series of waves always just about to break.
Too late to examine the small intestine

never mind swab vitreous potassium off an eyeball.
Too late to take in firsthand
the impression left on a sticker-photo-booth wall
of that great world at which this one may merely hint. Merely
    hint.

v

Too late to luxuriate in an *onsen*, or "communal bath made of
    cypress,"
and ponder an Elastoplast
that must have covered some minor bruise
winking from the depths. Too late to send it back to the analyst

with a swatch of sackcloth
or a panty-hose shred or a straight hair from her braid.
Too late to don a latex glove
and examine the corduroy road with its maggot brood

that traces itself back to the days of the Tokugawa shogunate
when Mount Fuji itself was coming to a head.
Who knew the body is a footnote
to the loss of its own heat

and the gases released when it begins to disintegrate
underlie a protruding tongue?
Too late to retrieve from the *onsen* in the shape of a giant gourd
that smelled like a lab's formaldehyde tank

her fancy-freighted skull that scarcely made a dent
in the pillow from which only buckwheat would now ever sprout.
Too late to divine from her stomach contents
the components of a metaphor that must now forever remain
    quite separate.

VI

It was far too late to reconstruct the train station bento box
she bought at Kyoto-eki the night before the night she took her
    vows
and threw up in the hollyhocks.
Too late to figure out if the Tokugawa clan would refuse

a plainclothes escort
to a less than fully fledged geisha.
Too late to insist that the body of a poem is no less sacred
than a temple with its banner gash

though both stink to high heaven.
Who knew that Budai is often confused with the Buddha?
Too late to divine
that what was now merely the air pocket of a capsized boat

had been a poem decomposing around a quill.
Too late to chart the flow
of purge fluid from a skull
that scarcely made a dent in the old buckwheat pillow

despite the metaphor that might have sustained her in her sorrow
as she, too, attempted to buck
this tiresome trend and alighted at the new station at Kazamatsuri
and felt, for the first time in years, the wind at her back.

VII

Whereas one might still try to reconcile the incorporeal
poem to the image of a fleshed-out Columbanus in a communal
    bath
his *Regula Monachorum*, or "Monastic Rule,"
hardly extended to the girl in the sticker-photo booth

who was yet to board the bullet train.
It was far too late to establish the interval
between her being so blissfully carefree and so balefully carrion.
Too late to deduce from the life cycle of a blowfly

a scenario that would not beggar
description less belief. Whereas I recognized the steel blue of one
    Musca
vomitoria, I couldn't connect the girl from the *purikura*
with the steel-blue mask

her sticker photo showed the world. The blowflies so few and far
    between
their threat must have seemed thinly veiled
until it was far too late to separate kimono and patten
from the black-green purge fluid.

Too late for the Tokugawa clan to send a galloper
over the bony ridge
in her skull with his accurate-to-within-a-thousandth-of-an-inch
    calipers
to report back to Edo on this security breach.

VIII

It was far too late to determine if these humors had been dry
    or wet
now I'd forsworn laying myself open
to the globefish. Too late to dissuade
the girl in the *purikura* from risking the type of panty-hose heel
    known as "Cuban"

never mind warning her off a Hi-Chew flavored with durian.
Far too late to inquire
why a poem had taken a wrong turn
on a corduroy road across a quaking mire

to have its own little meltdown.
I'd read somewhere that however advanced the art
of forensics has become, including the potassium analysis of
    the gelatin
in the vitreous humor, to fix the time of death is hard

if not hopeless. *Waxahachie.* Some propose the name means
    "fat wildcat"
while others persevere
in thinking "buffalo creek" or even "buffalo chips" just as good.
All I had to go on was the pouring of sulfur

over a clog print in snow, which seemed to highlight
that the poem began to self-digest
about the time I recognized that the sanitaria in which the
    lepers had been held
were nowhere in that great world of which this one is a sulfur
    cast.

IX

All I had to go on was the hunch that pupae would assail
the girl from the sticker-photo booth at the same rate as a poem
   cadaver.
Who knew that *lepis* meant "fish scale"?
All I had to go on was that a globefish would have gained its livor

once it, too, was kitted out for the slab.
Whereas I'd read somewhere that the mean
annual temperature on Mount Fuji's slopes
was −7 degrees centigrade, it was nonetheless too late to
   determine

if the humors of Hakone had been wet or dry.
Sanguine or phlegmatic. Choleric or melancholic.
In a drawer at the mortuary
a quail egg

from her railway-station bento
suggests the rate of cooling will vary by only a few degrees.
I'd read somewhere that the need for ID at the checkpoint
in Hakone started the sticker-photo craze

as far back as the Edo period. Along with the Japanese straight
    perm.
Who knew that geisha is often confused with *geiko*?
All I had to go on was a single maggot puparium
to help me substantiate the date of a corduroy road over a quag.

OHRWURM

Just as I'm loading up on another low carb pork rind snack
I spot in my wing-fuselage connection a fatigue crack.
It bears out my suspicion this low-level hum's a soundtrack
and everything I've seen so far I've seen so far in flashback.

LOVE POEM WITH PIG

When the people of Smartno threw their very last pig to the
    Turks
who had for months beset their hilltop town
they were gratified to look down
next morning and find the siege works
abandoned. Only stout defenders, the Turks concluded, would
    conjoin
blasphemy with beneficence. The way you poke a fork
at a slab of pork
shoulder or pork loin
on which you've yet to put your stamp
suggests you might succumb if my steadfastness were itself to
    fail.
Before you undermine
my confidence so I suddenly decamp
and go looking for some other hilltop town to assail
maybe you'll toss me a little something? Maybe you'll give me
    a sign?

@

Like the whorl of an out-of-this-world ear that had been lent
to an oak gall wasp by a tenth-century Irish monk
who would hold out oak gall ink against the predicament
in which he found himself . . .

                      Like the ever-unfolding trunk
of the elephant in the room that gives such a bad vibe
it vies with your old hippie girlfriend who once lent such weight
to any argument to which you feared she might subscribe,
including her insistence we abbreviate
our most promising rlshps . . .

                        Like the scrolled-down tail
of a capuchin monkey drawing on its inner strengths
as it hammers shortsighted snail against shortsighted snail
that has nonetheless gone to extraordinary lengths . . .

Like the tapeworm swallowed by a hippie who once was fat
but is now kind of bummed out you've lost track of where she's at.

LINES FOR THE QUATERCENTENARY OF

THE VOYAGE OF THE *HALVE MAEN*

Once Henry Hudson dreamed of breaking through
by his resolve alone, of homing in with all his navigational skill
on that Cathay just out of view,

a Cathay that lay due
north of the Lenni-Lenape's "Island of Many Hills."
What Henry Hudson dreamed of breaking through

was less the recalcitrance of his crew
than a sense the world was coming to a standstill.
In that Cathay just out of view

the Lenape would no longer make do
with a hart-heartened bluff, a shad-shadowed kill,
but dream with Henry Hudson they might indeed break through

the surface of things and hew
to this latest line of grist- and lumber mills.
From that Cathay just out of view

they might bring back a root-balled persimmon that grew
to the point at which it would now fulfill
all Henry Hudson dreamed of breaking through—

the idyll of our tattooed kids, our replica canoe,
mail-order venison conjuring from our grill
a Cathay just out of view

while we shrug off each new
Halve Maen bearing down on us, shrug it off by force of will,
as Henry Hudson dreamed of breaking through
to that Cathay just out of view.

YUP

A bottlenose dolphin opens *The Constraints*
of Desire to a passage she'd just as soon expunge.
Though she might lunge away from such morbid strains
she refuses to throw in the sponge.
A forensic entomologist examines a corpse
that's little more than a stain.
How long it's lain in the copse
is precisely what she wants to ascertain.
The forensic entomologist knows better than to plunge
into the contents of dead men's crops.
The bottlenose dolphin always rolls with the punch
when she finds herself against the ropes.
The forensic entomologist admits to some margin of error.
The bottlenose dolphin holds herself up to a mirror.

EXTRAORDINARY RENDITION

I

I gave you back my claim on the mining town
and the rich vein we once worked,
the tumble down
from a sluice box that irked

you so much, the narrow gauge
that opened up to one and all
when it ran out at the landing stage
beyond the falls.

I gave you back oak ties,
bully flitches, the hand-hewn crossbeams
from which hung hardtack

in a burlap bag that, I'd surmise,
had burst its seams
the last night we lay by the old spur track.

11

You gave me back your frown
and the most recent responsibility you'd shirked
along with something of your renown
for having jumped from a cage just before it jerked

to a standstill, your wild rampage
shot through with silver falderals,
the speed of that falling cage
and the staidness of our canyon walls.

You gave me back lake skies,
pulley glitches, gully pitches, the reflected gleams
of two tin plates and mugs in the shack,

the echoes of love sighs
and love screams
our canyon walls had already given back.

THE FLING

The shower that once lavished itself on you
and me in that studio off the Grand Concourse
and which we imagined would see us through
needles all the more for having lost its force.

BALLS

The last to go at the party, the first to head for the hills,
so used to sitting on the fence
these love nuts, these eggs, these pills
have seemed about as likely to dispense

themselves across the counter
as give short weight
by tipping their own scales. For the mounter
of the witness stand to differentiate

between the high-toned
Generalissimo and the general factotum
is for the worm

to cut the plow. It looks as if it's either been phoned
in from the front line, the scrotum,
or palmed off on us by the ancient or the infirm.

The ancient or the infirm only could have owned
such a wizened, "Please exhale,"
through-the-wringer wad. A brace of deboned
quail

and an *insalata caprese*. Then Vasselli happened on this teeny-
    weeny
third ball. Even though it was every bit as big
as one of those *bocconcini*
he assured me I shouldn't give a fig

about this sudden outgrowth
on my otherwise even keel.
Though I generally err

on the side of optimism I was loath
to fall in with a doctor who deemed this merely a spermatocele
and not a tumor—"Not a tumor, I swear."

III

I swear as a Roman supposedly swore an oath
on his balls and went through some Roman rigmarole
to ward off the behemoth
and its tail that stiffened like a cedar pole

in the book of Job. I listened to the gobblers
while they shook their wattles
and talked a load of old cobblers
about my youth, how I once built a house of bottles

and lived there like a toff,
how my passion for being toffish
extended to having my suits made by Henry Poole

where a cutter told me, with a little cough,
that while both are inclined to be standoffish,
the left ball hangs lower than the right as a general rule.

IV

In 85% of all cases, it seems, a cutter steers his trough
by a red light to the port.
When she sees you trying to make off
the modern woman is likely to have you up in court

not because you're an absconder
but because you don't have a point to press.
Now I'm propped up here I ponder
how I once put an ear to the keyhole dress

of that, ahem,
continuity girl with a thing about physical fitness.
It was she I first heard mourn

the loss of Latin, the loss of a sense of the Latin root and stem
that would help us weigh in on which came first—be it *testis* as
     "witness"
or *testis* as the "ball" on which the oath was sworn.

V

The oath I've sworn is that I won't condemn
these ball-broodings out of hand, given how one might yet
have it in it to cough up a little phlegm.
Once, of course, it was a jet

no less admired by continuity girls than butterfly wranglers.
Now I'm propped up in an open-back hospital gown
surrounded by doom hasteners and hope danglers.
Should you attend my final meltdown

and be inclined to speak ill
of me in my general vicinity, just remember how in the muddle
of General Anesthesia and General Factotum and Il Generalissimo

and their hushed recounting of my youthful thrills and spills
that, of all the senses in a huddle
round the bed, my hearing will be the last to go.

A MAYFLY

A mayfly taking off from a spike of mullein
would blunder into Deichtine's mouth to become Cuchulainn,
Cuchulainn who had it within him to steer clear
of a battlefield on the shaft of his own spear,
his own spear from which he managed to augur
the fate of that part-time cataloguer,
that cataloguer who might yet transcend the crush
as its own tumult transcends the thrush,
the thrush that's known to have tipped off avalanches
from the larch's lowest branches,
the lowest branches of the larch
that model themselves after a triumphal arch,
a triumphal arch made of the femora
of a woman who's even now filed under *Ephemera*.

THE WATERCOOLER

They're poisoning the atmosphere
now you and I've split,
coming out of the dark
to make those acid remarks
to all and sundry
because they're trying to get something clear.
The mistletoe puts up its mitts

now you and I've split.
The black oaks jostle
bark on careworn bark
to make those acid remarks
at the Christmas party
and the mistletoe puts up its mitts
to vie for the sweet-throated throstle

where the black oaks jostle
over a back fence
in the industrial park.
As they make those acid remarks
in the third-floor Ladies
and vie for the sweet-throated throstle,
the black oaks seem no less tense

over a back fence
than the chestnuts dishing the dirt.
Even the sweet-throated lark
will make those acid remarks
to all and sundry,
seeming no less tense
than so many introverts,

than the chestnuts dishing the dirt
down by the watercooler
about our being found stark
naked in the copy room. Such acid remarks
at the Christmas party.
Like so many introverts,
like all the other carpoolers

down by the watercooler,
the chestnuts cough up their lungs
and hint that it's only the payroll clerks
would make such acid remarks
in the third-floor Ladies.
Like all those other carpoolers,
the maples wag their tongues

and cough up their lungs
because they're trying to get something clear.

Something about our rekindling the spark
being the burden of their acid remarks
to all and sundry.
The maples wag their tongues.
They're poisoning the atmosphere.

LOSS OF SEPARATION: A COMPANION

In the province of Gallia Narbonensis and the
region of Nemausus there is a marsh called Latera
where dolphins and men co-operate to catch fish.

PLINY THE ELDER, *Natural History*

I used to think that *Mutual Aid*
had given rise to the first kibbutzim.
Now an economic blockade
seems merely a victimless crime.

I used to think I'd got it right
when I notched up a '59 Plymouth fin.
Now I fight only to fight
shy of the assembly line

where I'm waiting for some lover
to kick me out of bed
for having acted on a whim

after I've completely lost the thread
and find myself asking a river
to run that by me one more time.

A HUMMINGBIRD

At Nora's first post-divorce Labor Day bash
there's a fluster and a fuss and a fidget
in the fuchsia bells. "Two fingers of sour mash,
a maraschino cherry." "So the digit's
still a unit of measurement?" "While midgets
continue to demand a slice of the cake."
"A vibrator, you know, *that* kind of widget."
Now a ruby-throated hummingbird remakes
itself as it rolls on through mid-forest brake.
"I'm guessing she's had a neck lift *and* lipo."
"You know I still can't help but think of the *Wake*
as the apogee, you know, of the typo."
Like an engine rolling on after a crash,
long after whatever it was made a splash.

A SECOND HUMMINGBIRD

Yet another money man
with a finger in the till
at Flavor & Fragrance, my own
not standing still

no less a stance
than his, the only grounds
for his existence
now being to make such rounds

and roundelays as mine, to touch
what I've come to see
as the raw nerve

in each of us, each
doomed to think himself ever so
slightly behind some curve.

THE SIDE PROJECT

I

Forty years of Jumbo doing a one-handed handstand while some
    geek
simultaneously bites the head off a Wyandotte cock
and the band plays a Hungarian dance by Brahms
doesn't mean we're all on the same page. No Human Skeleton or
    Bearded Lady will primp
less for a small show than a great. A unicorn may graze
the dunes in all their vagaries
and never quite grasp the point
its horn is secured by Bondo.
Though a Norwegian bareback artiste may extend her liking for
    mere glogg
to mulled wines in general, a curl of the upper lip is a sign of colic
fairly specific to horses. Our impulse to give anything a try
takes in both sudatory
and Psalter, don't you know? I know from your well-documented
    propensity to moan
that your page would be very far from mine
even in the first of those *Syllabi*
Errorum Pope Pius IX, poor slob,
one-handedly set down in 1864, the very year Forepaugh first put
    a unicorn in clover
and Sherman's march to the sea meant the Civil War was pretty
    much over.

103

11

Forty years since we set up winter quarters in Florida and the
    hay bale
first tumbled into the economy of scale,
what with the cost
per unit going down as surely as an elephant will be gussied
up for the "come in." Arachne swallowing a sword all the way to
    the hilt
as the crowd inches into the tent. The frost now having taken
    such a hold
the citrus crop is under threat. Each orange and lemon moving
    in its own sphere.
As for the ignominies suffered by Lucifer,
a four-horned goat
who found himself frozen out by the big cat
contingent from their big car, they stab me in the heart.
Who hasn't woken up screaming in a four-poster elephant herd?
When we fell in love, the consequences for the Human Skeleton
and the Bearded Lady who operates a printers' guillotine
were simply dire.
Now Arachne is wearing what looks like ecclesiastical attire.
She hauls herself up through the rigging while the big cats
    adjourn
to their big caravan to ponder the laws of exponential decay and
    exponential return.

Forty years ago we realized that our impulse to be open
to pretty much anything may not run to the Feejee Mermaid
   (half-guppy, half-gibbon)
any more than a dead saint who may still sweat
the Precious Blood so beloved of Pius IX, poor sod.
I imagine Barnum taking umbrage
at the suggestion he'd staged Sherman's march
as a diversionary tactic. The unicorn Forepaugh turned out has
   the clover slobbers.
The umbrella-mouth gulper
is an eel that can take in damn nearly an entire clover field
but, like yourself, probably doesn't perform fellatio
and probably isn't impressed by an unbitten
Wyandotte's felt head with its eye still bright as a button
the geek holds up to the incoming crowd. That same
   Hungarian dance music
by Brahms. It's pretty clear Sherman was heading for Moscow
the way he eased his way with pig grease
even before the carpetbaggers
would reveal themselves most by what they most revile.
At least everyone in a circus crowd accepts he's no more than
   part of the rank and file.

Forty years from the first time we heard the strains of that
    Hungarian
dance by Brahms and did our best not to picture Jumbo hit by
    an unscheduled freight train
in a marshalling yard in Ontario, Arachne was making straight
    the path
over a mud bath
while Sherman gathered his unruly
troops with a drumroll
usually associated with a firing squad. You and I had hardly gone
    beyond our first peck
at a Coney Island frankfurter stand when I spotted the
    Norwegian bareback
artiste with one foot on the unicorn sire
and one on Barnum, as we'd come to know the chief impresario.
While the spotlight would ballyhoo
in a figure eight over an elephant folio
poster announcing General Tom Thumb and Jenny Lind, the
    Swedish Nightingale,
the Bearded Lady never lost her cool.
Arachne's insistence that an aerialist is not an acrobat

but a fallen angel serves only to perpetuate
your idea that manna from heaven
may be found to an unprecedented degree in Gray's Papaya at
　　Eighth Avenue and West Thirty-seventh.

Forty years to the day when a trawl through Jumbo's stomach
    would have brought up keys,
nuts, screws, washers, bolts, brass tacks, geegaws,
a bag of coins with which Judas Iscariot
had been bought off for his part in the papal masquerade
by that poor sod Barnum, or Dan Rice,
complete with performing pig. You and I know what it is to have
    a protective layer of ice
to stave off that greater freeze, know that it's not an out-and-out
    hoax
when the Bearded Lady enters the blade box
to be sawn in half. That may not be a spurt
of blood as such but we know this is no less a blood sport
than when Arachne ran into a little impediment as the crowd
    inched into the tent.
Our impulse to apply yellow Centaur Liniment
to Jumbo or his cousin, Toung
Taloung, was ill-founded, a wrinkling of the nose coupled with
    a looseness of the dung
being a sign of croup in the mahout. It was strictly of her own
    accord

the Bearded Lady was cut into quarto
and bound in stillborn calf hide
like your run-of-the-mill Feegee Mermaid or Pickled Punk
   malformed in his formaldehyde.

Forty years of Barnum trying to establish the cost per unit of
    promoting Commodore Nutt
as the new Tom Thumb, of Arachne working without a safety net
at any moment likely to foreground the rot
in erotica. What must have made Arachne finally see red
was the realization that, at the 1846 Papal Conclave,
Pius IX had overseen the Bearded Lady being sawn in half
by the moderate and conservative factions. For it would surely not
    be lost
on Pius IX that an aerialist
is no mere acrobat, given his powers
of infallibility, don't you know? Forty years of Jumbo showing
    his prowess
in the one-handed handstand
while some geek simultaneously decapitates a rooster. The tune
    that will come to haunt
me as Lucifer leads the "come in" and the geek spits the head
    into the front stalls
will rise above the big cat calls.
It's that same old Hungarian dance tune
played on a cornet from a unicorn that once grazed the dunes
in all their vagaries. We took it as a signal for Frog Boy and the
    Human Chimera to wreak
vengeance on Barnum for being such an out-and-out control freak.

Forty years to the day since Sherman set off from Atlanta for
    Savannah with his big caravan
of big cats, top dogs, a performing pig named Lord Byron and,
    no less proven
in battle, the Missing Link, Frog Boy,
the Human Chimera and the Human Alligator. Barnum still
    insisting this isn't a decoy
to distract us from some main event. Your insisting, meanwhile,
    this was chalk
from Arachne's hands on my pants. Some days it looked as if
    Lucifer might stalk
a raggedy-ass lion
to pull down the news from behind the headline.
It was 1867 when the frankfurter trend
took off on Coney Island and it must indeed have marked the end
of an era to a goat with four horns,
never mind the first unicorn
Forepaugh had turned out under the unicorn nomenclature.
The Missing Link and the Human Alligator
now found themselves going off behind the generator truck
to work up their new trick
while I found myself checking for symptoms of croup
in both the Norwegian bareback artiste and Arachne, then the
    new girl in the trapeze troupe.

VIII

Forty years of Forepaugh or Dan Rice or Barnum IX heaping
    ignominy
upon ignominy really doesn't mean
we're all of a like mind as to how to deal with the rash
of pickpockets at a matinee, never mind the crash
in the marshalling yard in Ontario that thrust my little side
    project front and center.
Jumbo would no more truly benefit from Centaur
Liniment than, in the Civil War, Barnum truly brought cheer
to the country with a Pickled Punk in a Mason jar.
It was in Ontario the Norwegian bareback artiste's triumphing
    over Arachne
as she might over an unbroken
Appaloosa came to a sudden halt. Now the Missing Link
    prevailed over *Dictatus Papae*
in the way Gray's Papaya
has prevailed over Papaya King.
I know your propensity for believing Barnum was no more
    subsumed by Ringling
than Lee was routed by Sherman's Savannah campaign
but you've got to admit the "come in"
is an effective way of consigning a crowd to the peripheries.
It was in Ontario you and I would first find a way of staving off
    that even greater freeze.

Forty years after I stumbled upon the Norwegian bareback
    artiste, herself without a stitch,
helping Barnum to make a pitch
for the upcoming gigs at Gethsemane and Golgotha, I found
    Arachne forcing mere
glogg down the Good Thief's throat. Forepaugh, meanwhile,
    in an unpublished memoir,
would admit to having hired the gang of pickpockets
that fleeced the matinee crowd. I imagine you as a mahout lying
    under a spigot
in Coney Island and wrinkling your nose
as you pull down the news
behind the headline that you've finally had your first peck of a
    frankfurter.
Forty years since we set up winter quarters
in Florida and the Bearded Lady was cut into duodecimo,
not even the elephant folio could subsume
Tom Thumb and Jenny Lind the way Sherman took in Atlanta.
What you found on my pants on Coney Island
wasn't chalk but rosin, don't you know? I suppose that, prior to
    the St. Louis hippodrome,

the hope had been that Arachne's spiking her red wine with equal
    parts rum
and potato akvavit
might allow her to bounce off the Appaloosa's rosin-dappled
    safety net and land on her feet.

x

Forty years since Sherman was attacked by Confederate guerillas
    from the rear
and you and I first settled into our starring roles in our own little
    raree
show cum snake-oil
circus it's pretty clear we've found a way to foil
most guerilla attacks by making a preemptive strike on the
    "citrus crop."
I'm no more interested in an Arachne showing me the ropes
than in a Norwegian bareback artiste and her umbrella-mouth
    gulper eel.
I imagine a Norwegian bareback artiste, as recently as 1864,
    setting the papal seal
on a Mason jar in which is suspended the first (and last) *Syllabus
Errorum.*
Who hasn't woken up screaming in a forest of four-poster
    pachyderms
where thin-skinned mahouts from their howdahs
incite us to winter in Florida?
The joint funeral of the Norwegian bareback artiste trampled by
    her Appaloosa
and Arachne, who fell to her death in a hippodrome in St. Louis,

reminds us no Bearded Lady nor Human Skeleton will prink
less than the Human Alligator or Missing Link
for if Jumbo succumbing to a rogue train in a marshalling yard
    truly marks the end of an era
it also truly allows us to remake ourselves as Frog Boy and the
    Human Chimera.

THE SOD FARM

Her car must have caught fire
when she missed a turn
or blew a tire,
the girl with third-degree burns

who slammed into a tree
by the mist-shrouded sod farm.
40%. Third degree.
Her gauze-wrapped arms

now taking in unending variations
and surprises: temples, grottoes,
waterfalls, ruins, leafy glades

with sculpture, and such features
as would set off the imagination
on journeys in time as well as space.

A PORCUPINE

Simply because she'd turn her back on me,
a porcupine on the Homer Noble farm
would unwittingly
give me a shot in the arm,

bustling off in her ball gown
while clutching a quillwork purse.
I'm thinking how our need to do ourselves down
will often be in inverse

proportion to how much we want
to be esteemed. I'm thinking of those who,
in the same breath, will kiss up to us and kiss

us off. I'm thinking of a woman who'd flaunt
from her shoulder blade a tattoo:
I REGRET THIS.

ANOTHER PORCUPINE

Looking for all the world like smoke starting up from a skillet
and leaving in a huff
while hefty enough
to drag her pillow filled with buckwheat and millet
from the Dumpster behind the Five-and-Dime,
another porcupine would tough

it out from the industrial quarter
by way of a six-foot drop
to the redemption bay of the Co-op
where she did double duty as a can and bottle sorter.
Soda lime . . . Aluminum . . . Soda lime . . .
Looking for all the world like the last prop

that had kept my car's low-beam tunnel
from falling about my head
she dragged me after her, in dread,
to where she'd funnel
herself into a parking lot. I imagined her climb
through the window of a shed

in search of an odd work glove, a sandal,
any haft or helve remotely worth its salt,
choosing to exalt

over the pristine a sweat-cured handle
clearly past its prime,
favoring any with which I'd long since have found fault

and consigned to the midden
alongside everything else that had managed to fail.
The parking lot was now less track than mountain trail
through which I followed her, unbidden,
towards the sublime
of a snowcapped newspaper bale

that lay not in *Recycling* but the bin marked *Waste Matter*,
there to be broken down and burned.
Like so many who've yearned
to find a pattern in the blood spatter
at the scene of a crime,
spurred on as we are by the very thing we've spurned,

this porcupine seemed set to plummet
towards every barb we've hurled—
seeking out through the low cloud that swirled
about the summit
only a plot marked by a spade shaft, its ingrained grease and grime,
where once she'd gone looking for all the world.

CAPRICCIO IN E MINOR FOR

BLOWFLY AND STRINGS

FOR JOHN ASHBERY

Sometimes a wind is content to wrap itself in the flag
where it was once inclined to raise
the roof by, albeit discreetly, loosening a ridge tile
here and there. This was before discretion became the better part
of the fire-resistant velour of modern car upholstery. Not even
    the burning of a tire
around a woman's neck may effect as much change

as a flaying Swift witnessed near the Bristol Corn Exchange.
Now all vessels intending to proceed through the bridge must
    show a flag
by day and at night a white light. It seems all youthful rebels tire
of their youthful spirits, spirits we used to raise
with the art-house title sequence. Once Swift himself took the
    part
of a lyric ode's ability to slate, a catch to tile,

against Vanbrugh's blockbuster of modern wit and style
and exposed it to the elements. Sometimes maggots will fling
    their loose change
into the hat of a woman by the side of the road, a fiddler whose
    part

is notated here and there by a little flag
to remind her to try to raise
the emotional stakes. Sometimes a wind betokens the fact we
    never tire

of describing Swift as a master of satire
while leaving him for the most part unread. That Swift may have
    had a tile
loose is a topic no one much cares to raise
in this era of live and let loaf. Sometimes change for the sake of
    change
might not be the worst flag
under which to sail as when maggots, for their part,

are content to be in a crowd scene from which they'll nonetheless
    depart
about as gracefully as Swift would retire
from a debate on the slave trade. It seems all youthful spirits flag
where they were once so volatile.
Gone are the days when a wind would call for change
in an art-house way, hoping to raise

the level of debate above the producer paraphrase
to which we've now succumbed. Sometimes a maggot doesn't
    want a speaking part
like an animal "of largest size." Everything will change

for Troy as for Tyre
when it's doused in gasoline, like a woman dumped on a flame-
    retardant tile
by two carjackers who would flag

her down while pretending to change a tire.
Sometimes it's not enough for a wind to play its part and meekly
    take its turn in the turnstile.
Sometimes raising a flag isn't enough to raise a red flag.

WAYSIDE SHRINES

I

Doomed as I was to follow a big rig
laden with pigs and a wrecker with its intermittent strobe
I was all the more conscious of piles of rock
marking the scene of a crash,
some with handwritten notes, others a cache
of snapshots in a fogged-up globe.

Even a makeshift mobile may see off one of Calder's
and the path among the alders
pan out like a prom queen's occipital lobe,
yet nothing can confirm one's sense of being prized
like another's being anathematized.

11

Having myself been run out of town
I might easily have gone down on my knees
by each white cross or posy in its tin
and resigned myself to the fact
a cord of dead wood may be stacked
between two living trees.

Even an acorn tastes bitter
to the runt of the litter
when it begins to feel the squeeze
yet those pigs had seemed content
in their profound disgruntlement.

III

I might easily have followed the ruck
to where a utility truck hit a dry stone bank,
that red rag
a token of where its load
shifted and kicked off the beehive-hut episode
on which the narrative sank.

Even the lily plugging an oil filter
with its stem slightly out of kilter
has somehow succeeded in pulling rank
yet failed to lend much weight
to whatever it means to commemorate.

IV

A flower-pumped Pirelli tire
that comes across as part pyre, part tomb,
must have taken up a dare
from a wiper blade
that it could wholly fade
while hastening to bloom.

Even the spit splutter
of baby's breath against a sand-ribbed shutter
may look for all the world like spume
yet give no sign of the shoal where a prom queen would pit
herself against the indefinite.

V

Another plotline's come to rest
in a tool chest emblazoned with *Pro Tuff*
on which there roost
a molten fuse,
an ace of spades and a pair of twos
where somebody's called somebody's bluff.

Even a candleholder
on top of the offending boulder
speaks to a flame being snuffed
yet managing to live
while it's completely inoperative.

VI

Had I had more than a glimpse of a lake
through a break in a plateau,
had I not suddenly been forced to brake
for Apollo wrapped in polythene,
I might have been emboldened
and gone with the flow.

Even a road resists being led to water
like a lamb to the slaughter
at ISAAC'S TRUCK & TOW
yet smoke had risen with next to no fuss,
calm above the calamitous.

VII

Now as gas prices soared
another billboard had held out INJURED?
before it all but implored
1-888-WE-CAN-HELP.
I caught the yelp
from a clothesline of a plaid work shirt.

Even a bald-faced bullock may falter
as it mounts an altar
that's little more than a pile of dirt
yet a storm window took a stance
against what it must discountenance.

VIII

Whatever had once put us out of skew
now threw me for another loop
as I took in a sky
in which a couple of clouds had failed to catch
they'd never be a match
for that high-flying trapeze troupe.

Even those former self-inflators
who now fast on acorn meal and slaters
were distorted by the sky hoop
yet ironed themselves out through the prism
of early Irish monasticism.

These modern monks whose low self-worth
has them leave earth for a few years
know that not only a wreath
from a sacred grove
but a Styrofoam alcove
marks the spot where they went clear.

Even the ashes we scatter
and the plaques we set up tend to flatter
mostly their own engineers
yet the smashing of a radiator grille
may soothe the implacable.

X

I might easily have knelt
for this heartfelt lighting of a torch
where someone nailed it, or himself was nailed,
though the spot where we take a wrong turn
is rarely marked by either an urn
or a tire scorch.

Even a dog and pup, mother and daughter,
may half tote, half totter
their matching luggage from a porch
yet be ingrained with a sense they too readily press
the point of their devotedness.

XI

Dedicated as I was to getting the jump
on the big rig, the fact that a stump might still bleed
through a plaid shirt didn't chime
with just how little any of this counts
when not even the grain in the grain silo amounts
to chicken feed.

Even her momentary taking shelter
and finding some ease from the helter-skelter
offered the prom queen a glimpse of what it is to succeed
yet the sudden failure of a brake drum
extended her lease on Elysium.

ACKNOWLEDGMENTS

Acknowledgments are due to the editors of *Agenda, Alaska
Quarterly Review, The American Scholar, Answering Back* (Picador),
The Arts Show (RTE), *Atlantic Monthly, The Beckett Circle, Berkeley
Poetry Review, The Best American Poetry 2008* (Scribner), *The Best
of Irish Poetry 2009, The Best of Irish Poetry in English 2010,
Blackbox Manifold, Boulevard Magenta, Captivating Brightness*
(Ballynahinch), *The Clifden Anthology, Conduit, Earls Court, Five
Points, From the Small Back Room: A Festschrift for Ciaran Carson*
(Netherlea), *The Guardian, Harper's Magazine, Little Star,
Love Poet, Carpenter: Michael Longley at Seventy* (Enitharmon),
*The Manchester Review, Margie, McSweeney's, Mimesis, The Museum
as Muse* (Princeton University Art Museum), *The New Republic,
The New Yorker, The New York Review of Books, The New York Times,
PEN America, A Poetic Celebration of the Hudson River* (Carcanet),
*Poetry Daily, Poetry Salzburg Review, The Princeton University
Library Chronicle, Pushcart Prize XXXIV: Best of the Small Presses,
Pushcart Prize XXXV: Best of the Small Presses, Redivider, Round
Magazine, Stony Thursday Book, Sugar House Review, That Island
Never Found: Essays and Poems for Terence Brown* (Four Courts),
*TLS, TriQuarterly, Vallum, The Washington Post, Washington
Square Review, World Literature Today* and *The Yellow Nib*.
A number of poems were published in *When the Pie Was Opened*
(American University of Paris/Sylph Editions, 2008), *Plan B*
(Enitharmon, 2009) and *Wayside Shrines* (Gallery, 2009).